Ocean Colour Scene

by Joh

First published in Great Britain in 1997 by Chameleon Books
an imprint of Andre Deutsch Ltd
106 Great Russell Street
London WC1B 3LJ

Andre Deutsch Ltd is a subsidiary of VCI plc

Printed and bound in Great Britain by Butler and Tanner, Frome, Somerset.

A catalogue record for this book is available from the British Library
ISBN 0 233 99159 X

Ocean
Colour
Scene

Ocean Colour Scene
Ocean Colour Scene
Ocean Colour Scene

When **Ocean Colour Scene** appeared on the first-ever broadcast of Chris Evans's TFI Friday to perform their new single, Riverboat Song - which was to become the theme music to the weekly TV series - most of the audience assumed they were a brand-new band. Some probably knew that they were friends of Oasis, with whom they had already played several dates. A few might have known that they frequently made up the backing band for Paul Weller's live show. Nobody could have guessed that, despite the fact that the band themselves were calling Riverboat Song their debut single, precisely the same line-up of Ocean Colour Scene had not only put out several singles and an album in the past, but that they had already experienced the media hype of being hailed as the next big thing almost five years earlier.

Inspired (like Oasis) by seeing the Stone Roses play at the height of their success, Ocean Colour Scene formed in 1989. From their initial success and signing to a major label, through their years of contractual and financial problems to their rebirth, the band have never looked like splitting up. Their resurrection came on the back of their refusal to change either their name or their 60s-influenced style of music - however unhip both were taken to be. Those who knew of Ocean Colour Scene's past life probably didn't expect them to score a success second time around. They were undoubtedly, however, astonished by the band's determination and perseverance. Perhaps if they had known just how much Birmingham's Ocean Colour Scene had been through together, they wouldn't have given up hope. The four had not only spent years of their lives pursuing success, but also keeping each other sane during the lean times. From the moment they met, they knew that they shared musical tastes and ambitions unlike anybody else they had ever met. In fact, their lives and interests had followed similar paths right up to that fateful Stone Roses gig.

Ocean Colour Scene

Simon Fowler

Simon Fowler

SINGER

First band: The Fanatics

Biggest influences: The Beatles, The Velvet Underground, Stone Roses, Rolling Stones, Thin Lizzy, Neil Young, Free, The Beach Boys.

Interesting facts: one of his most treasured possessions is a Beatles watch, he can do near perfect impersonations of John Lennon and Frank Spencer.

Distinguishing features: oldest in the band at 31, he can often be overheard talking to himself.

Ocean Colour Scene

Steve Cradock

Steve Cradock

GUITARIST

First band: The Boys

Biggest influences: The Jam, Otis Redding,
Booker T And The MGs, The Isley Brothers, The
Beatles, Neil Young, Aretha Franklin, Tim Hardin

Interesting facts: he used to own Paul Weller's
scooter until it got nicked, he was rumoured in
The Daily Star to be dating Kathy Lloyd

Distinguishing features: youngest in the band at
26, he is always seen in slightly flared, 70's style
corduroy jeans and button-down Mod shirts.

Ocean Colour Scene

Damon Minchella

BASSIST

First band: The Fanatics

Biggest influences: The Beatles, Stevie Wonder, Bob Dylan, Small Faces, The Beach Boys, Northern Soul, The Who

Interesting facts: he got married in 1996, he spent his first royalty cheque from Moseley Shoals on a sports car, he loves the fact that The Riverboat Song has been used on Sportsnight.

Distinguishing features: the only designer dresser in the band.

Oscar Harrison

DRUMMER

First band: Echo Base

Biggest influences: The Small Faces, Sly Stone, UB40, The Beatles, The Rolling Stones, James Brown,

Interesting facts: his ambition is to live in a house boat and he is obsessed with gadgets and anything mechanical.

Distinguishing features: he is never seen without sunglasses (even in the dark), he is rarely heard talking, he has a penchant for knitted skull caps and he suffers badly from hay fever.

Chapter One

Even though Ocean Colour Scene are often said to have met for the first time at Birmingham's Irish Centre the night of the Stone Roses gig, they all knew each other by sight either from the local music circuit, or they were already playing in bands together. Singer Simon Fowler and bassist Damon Minchella had been members of a Velvet Underground influenced outfit called The Fanatics for some time. They had recently sacked their drummer and invited Oscar Harrison to join them. The fourth part of the equation was guitarist Steve Cradock, who had, a few months, earlier split from local mod band The Boys. In fact, it was the mod connection that linked the four even before they met. While the scene was actually subsiding around the country, the future members of Ocean Colour Scene refused to let their interest slide. Luckily, Birmingham, despite being renowned for its heavy-rock groups, retained several mod clubs and venues. There were even a clutch of local mod bands like The Moments, The Clique, The Aardvarks and The Immediate, who continued to play to their die-hard fans.

In fact, it was the **mod** connection that linked the four even before they met.

Once I decided I was going to be in a **band** there

Once I decided I was going to be in a band there

er any doubt that I would devote my **whole** life to it.

The Who On stage, when it's loud, you think it sounds like **The Who**. In reality, it sounds like fucki

Although he may not have realised it at the time, it was those bands that first inspired Steve Cradock. After a few years of bumming around in several no-hope outfits, Steve formed his first real band in 1988 with schoolfriends from his home town of Solihull, a suburb of south Birmingham. The band christened themselves The Boys and Steve switched from playing bass to guitar. He was still only 17.

'We were crap,' Steve told Record Collector, looking back. 'On stage, when it's loud, you think it sounds like The Who. In reality, it sounds like fuckin' Housemartins b-sides. We used to do loads of covers - all the ones The Jam did.'

The Boys played at various mod events, mostly covering 60s classics such as The Buzzcocks' Ever Fallen in Love With Someone, The Monkees' Pleasant Valley Sunday, The Clash's Should I Stay or Should I Go and, most notably, The Jam's Strange Town. Significantly, they also did versions of soul songs such as The Isley Brothers' This Old Heart of Mine.

The Boys' first London gig was at Covent Garden's Rock Garden. They then started coming to the capital to play well-known mod clubs such as The Bizz at the Royal Oak in Tooley Street. From there, they progressed to playing scooter rallies in the mod uniform of boating blazers and parkas. In

late 1988, they released an EP on their own label, under the guiding hand of Chris Cradock, the band's manager and also Steve's dad. It was called Happy Days.

'We just did it ourselves, got it pressed up and sold it at gigs,' Steve later told Record Collector. 'The label didn't even have a name. The single came in a black and white sleeve with a really horrible picture on the cover. We sold it at scooter rallies, too.'

The Boys' only other recorded output was a track that they contributed to a compilation on London mod label, Unicorn. Their biggest claim to fame, however, was the fact that they got to support former Small Faces frontman Steve Marriott at a concert he played at Birmingham's Irish Centre.

'That night was the first time I ever smoked drugs,' Steve confessed to Record Collector. 'Steve Marriott was ace. We sat on the side of the stage and chatted afterwards. He really knew how to enjoy himself.'

Around that time, a Derby-based fanzine called Empty Hours is reported to have hailed Cradock as one of the best new songwriters in Birmingham. It also revealed that major record label Polydor was interested in signing them. Despite the fact that attention was beginning to grow for the band outside their tiny local circuit, by the start of the

as b-sides.
ns b-sides. fuckin' Housemartins b-sides.
On stage, when it's loud, you think it sounds like **The Who**. In reality, it sounds like fuckin' Housemartins b-sides.

following year, The Boys had ceased to exist.

Just months later, Steve attended the Stone Roses gig that was to change his life. Significantly, at exactly the same concert were The Fanatics, a Velvet Underground influenced indie guitar band. Fronted by singer Simon Fowler, the four-piece already boasted two more future Ocean Colour Scene members in bassist Damon Minchella and drummer Oscar Harrison. Damon had been in the band since it started. Oscar was drafted in to replace The Fanatics' female drummer, whom they had recently ousted.

'We got rid of her because she wasn't very good,' Damon later told Record Collector. 'She was called Caroline Bullock - and you can't have a drummer called that! I remember us all going to see the Wonder Stuff in Birmingham when their first album came out - we formed around that time.'

Newly recruited drummer Oscar's background was with an 11-strong reggae collective called Echo Base, who had been signed to UB40's label. After releasing their debut album and touring Britain with UB40, however, Echo Base appeared to be making no commercial headway. It was through their manager, who also worked occasionally for The Fanatics, that Oscar first met Simon and Damon. He soon quit Echo Base to join their band.

The Fanatics released just one 12" single, called

Suburban Love Songs, on local indie label Chapter 22. In Record Collector, Simon described the single as 'a weak, watered-down record - like The Buzzcocks'.

'Nothing really happened,' recalled Damon in the same interview. 'We got a few local radio sessions and John Peel played the EP a few times. Nobody ever really got the business side together.'

Nevertheless, Simon - despite already having a day job as a reporter for local papers such as the Birmingham Post and the Mail - knew that his destiny lay in music.

'Once I decided I was going to be in a band,' he told Time Out, 'there was never any doubt that I would devote my whole life to it. But for ages, I never considered music as a sort of job thing, because the only musicians I really knew were The Beatles. And to aspire to be them was just patently ridiculous.

'Football was the only other love in my life. I used to play Subbuteo endlessly, even on my own. The reason I became a journalist was because I wanted to be a football commentator. My uncle used to work on a local paper in Norwich with John Motson, so John Motson became my hero. I've no doubt that if I'd continued in journalism, that's what I would have done.'

Before they had an opportunity to put out any

Having turned down an Andy Weatherall rem
predicted **NME**, 'Ocean Colour Scene put themselves ahead of the ba
bunch by being obstinate and **unique.**

more records, The Fanatics attended the fateful Stone Roses gig, independently of Steve Cradock. It took place at the Irish Centre in Birmingham in the summer of 1989.

'Everything felt so optimistic,' Cradock later told Q magazine. 'You kept thinking your head was in the past or something, but the Roses changed that totally. You could be in a new group who were into older stuff and still feel current.'

Needless to say, the concert had the same effect on Simon and his band as it did on Steve. So impressed were all three by Ian Brown and the rest of the Manchester band that they decided to adopt similar 60s influences. Having got to know Steve from the local music circuit, they asked him to replace the guitarist in their newly revitalised band and renamed themselves Ocean Colour Scene.

'I already knew Simon from around Solihull,' Steve told Record Collector recently. 'The Fanatics were into the Velvet Underground vibe. I used to watch them in their Blondie suits and think, yeah, I identify with that. And then they wore army stuff and Simon had his Rickenbacker guitar and beret. I was well into it.'

There was, however, a more personal, family reason that would tie Simon and Steve together for years in the future.

'What connects me and Steve is something that goes far beyond other groups,' Simon later told NME. 'I mean, my old man was a policeman for 30 years and so was Steve's. But his dad was in the Special Branch, protecting the Prime Minister and stuff like that, and mine was a lot more to do with the day-to-day stuff. And I think that kind of helped us, because we have both fought against doing things that we were supposed to. My first ambition was always to be a football commentator, and so when I left school, I became a journalist because I thought that one day I might get to do what I always wanted. But really I was just doing what my parents expected of me, you know.'

As soon as Simon saw the Stone Roses that night, he began actively to work towards what he wanted for the first time. Fired up by the exciting new wave of so-called 'baggy' bands such as the Happy Mondays that were coming out of Manchester at the time, Ocean Colour Scene started writing in earnest and rehearsing their songs in the converted garage of the Cradock family home. It was a good time for young, northern guitar bands with the willingness to work to form. In the wake of the Stone Roses' massive critical success, record companies based in London were about to begin signing any half-decent hopefuls for ridiculous sums of money. Doubtless aware of this, former Beat and Fine Young Cannibals manager John Mostyn noticed a spark of something special in

Ocean Colour Scene after witnessing their first-ever gig at the Stoke Wheatsheaf. Little over six months after they had formed, he signed them up to a new independent Birmingham label that he had just formed. It was called !Phffft.

In September 1990, Ocean Colour Scene released a well-received debut single, Sway, an R&B-influenced tune that perfectly captured the dancefloor-friendly guitar sound of the times. It was also enough to earn the band an appearance on the first-ever broadcast of Channel 4's The Word and a top spot in NME's end-of-year hot tips for 1991, alongside the Manic Street Preachers, Real People, Top, Anastasia Screamed and a host of so-called shoe-gazing bands such as Thousand Yard Stare and Moose.

'Having turned down an Andy Weatherall remix,' predicted NME, 'Ocean Colour Scene put themselves ahead of the baggy bunch by being obstinate and unique. Sexy and sullen, they'll prove once and for all that the culture that spawned them was not a flash in the pan but a major landmark, by putting out the only LP that matters this year.'

Of the crop of - admittedly - lame new bands to have formed on the back of the success of the Stone Roses, OCS were easily the best. Not only did they look the part (as committed mods, they cared about their clothes, shoes and hairstyles), they were also the most technically proficient and they possessed, in singer Simon Fowler, a handsome, attention-grabbing frontman. Add to that the enthusiasm within the industry over rock records that could cross over into the clubs (not to mention among the young, British record-buying public), and it was scarcely surprising that major labels soon began bidding to sign up the band.

It was Phonogram that won the war, although Ocean Colour Scene now claim that they would have preferred to develop on a small label before being thrust into the corporate, profit-obsessed world of the major record companies.

'Unknown to us,' Damon told Record Collector, '!Phffft Records did a licensing deal with Fontana and basically sold us for £600,000, and we didn't see a penny of it. !Phffft had a couple of other bands, and a lot of Fontana's money, which was supposed to come to us, was spent on their albums, which were never released because Fontana just wanted us. Yesterday Today came out listing both labels and went in at No 49, which we were chuffed about.'

Simon's additional comments showed how strongly he felt about what happened.

'!Phffft basically sold us right down the fuckin' river. We liked the idea of being on an indie label just to get our musical act going. All of a sudden, we're on a major label. It was very confusing.'

Chapter Two

After the indie-label success of the debut single Sway, the press began to pick up on Ocean Colour Scene. The band conducted interviews in the impressive, Tudor-style offices of !Phffft in their home town of Solihull. What they didn't realise at the time was that !Phffft had just sold the rights to release their records to Fontana for an alleged £350,000. The band never received any of the money, although they found themselves tied to a five-album deal with their new bosses.

The business dealings may have confused the band members, but it probably didn't worry them. Their future was looking too rosy to be anything other than optimistic. In a piece on new bands, NME called Simon a 'superstar in the making', not to mention a 'spaced-out sex monkey'. 'He has the looks, ego and motormouth to make a million,' was their opening shot.

'I don't know whether it's right to want to be stars,' Simon retorted. 'But the fact is we do, so there's no point getting hung up about it. James Dean knew how to be a star. Marilyn Monroe knew how to be a

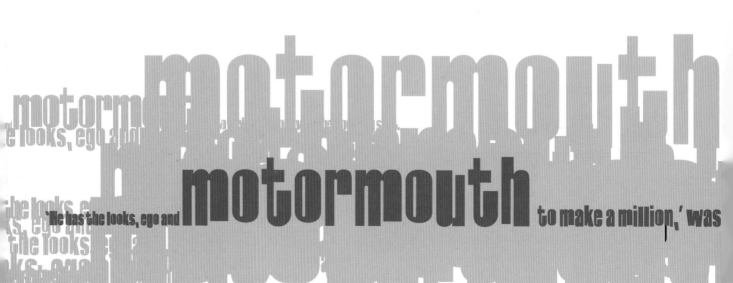

motormouth

'...to make a million,' was their opening shot.

ke a million,' was their opening shot.

ing shot. ...s their opening shot.

the problem is that **Ocean Colour Scene** are a wonderful Hall of Mirrors reflection of Brit guitar pop's most recent obsessions

erful Hall of Mir   tle

Right now nothing can stain his charisma because the other half of the reason, the music his band make, is firing on all cylinders.

star. So does Tim Burgess. He knows his looks are probably more important than his voice. The whole of pop culture is about images. Joni Mitchell is a great songwriter, but she's not a great star. Same as Van Morrison. He's got the music but he's not Tim Burgess and he never will be. He always looks like he's just come out of a bank. The Who will always be a better band than The Kinks simply because they're a band with a stronger sense of image.'

'Simon Fowler is undoubtedly the star of OCS,' reasoned NME. 'His striking persona is half the reason why fortune came all over the band recently with a huge Phonogram record deal. Right now nothing can stain his charisma because the other half of the reason, the music his band make, is firing on all cylinders. Ideally, one suspects, he would like to be all the great stars he gushes over - Ziggy Stardust, Jagger, Richards, The Beatles - all rolled into one. In the relatively small sphere of pop consciousness, where OCS sit regally upon the throne, he is just that. Whether it be pontificating over lofty ideals or Jagger dancing about the stage, he never fails to come up with the grand gesture. "I'm just a song and dance man and we're just entertainers," he insists. More than that, in the world of next great white guitar groups, OCS - not unlike the Stone Roses two years ago - are the band tipped to be just that.'

Everything was set for the band's second single - an EP led by the track Yesterday Today - to propel them closer to their goal of pop stardom.

'Yesterday Today,' claimed NME, 'has a similar melodic rush and ecstatic feel as the Stone Roses' Elephant Stone. Awash with dandelion harmonies and spine-tingling guitar lines, it almost loses itself in 60s psychedelia. To their credit, it remains individual and fresh enough to leave the listener in no doubt about the decade whence it came. Ocean Colour Scene are young, hopelessly cool and waiting to happen.'

Not every journalist was as keen, however. Andrew Collins (who, as the editor of Q magazine, would put the band on the front cover years later) was far from convinced by Yesterday Today.

'I find myself strangely and mysteriously drawn to killing Ocean Colour Scene,' he wrote. 'This is an illogical, nay, fanciful urge since I have never really heard them. However, now I have listened to their first, Phonogram-fuelled 60s Baggle Taggle on vinyl, I find that I can't even be arsed to find out where they live. Seen it, done it. Bo-o-o-o-o-oring.'

Single of the Week went to The Poppy Factory and guest reviewers Soho wrote off Ocean Colour Scene as 'the baggy Hollies'.

Other critics wondered whether the band were

perhaps too retro.

'We've soaked up 35 years of pop culture,' said Simon, defending himself in NME. 'If we hadn't known what had gone before, we wouldn't know what to do. If you'd been brought up in some controlled experiment and never heard the past 30 years of music, would you know how to be in a band? I don't think we would.

'Almost every interview we've done, people go on about us being psychedelic. I don't think we are. The only definition of psychedelia is music fuelled by LSD. All our music has in common with that is its intensity.

'We have the definitive 60s guitar sound that dates back to Hendrix, Pete Townshend and George Harrison. We have vocal harmonies that were done in the 60s. The biggest link between us and the style of songs from that period, though, is the songwriting. We're the only band that can write songs as good as they were in the 60s. Certain bands use the 60s style of clothes and guitar sounds, but they'll never be able to write the songs. We can. And I can sing them.'

Ocean Colour Scene then set out on a Yesterday Today tour of Britain, which culminated in the band headlining an industry-sponsored week of up-and-coming bands at London's ICA in April.

'The superbly rehearsed Ocean Colour Scene - starring frontman Simon Fowler, the first real performer that Baggy-delia has thrown up - have reached an end point in the perfecting of the stratospheric-wash-of-meandering-paisley-guitar sound,' pontificated NME. 'Crescendos, lilting abstraction, wah-wah pedals - they have it all and they control it beautifully. Brian Jones-faced guitarist Stephen Cradock's backwards-jointed fingers bleed sitar-friendly drones over Oscar Harrison's scatter beats and Damon Minchella's hypno bass lines.

'Simon's voice is magnificently disembodied, fraying into histrionic screams at all the right moments. They have raspberry-ripple key changes and ethereal vocal harmonies of cathedral-choir standard. And the tunes are all ultra-vividly bold.

Tonight we get the extended versions, allowing Talk On to unfold, and Fly Me to shimmer enticingly. The propulsive Sway, already the band's anthem, is suitably fired up, and Yesterday Today and Another Girl's Name, from the current EP, are dazzling pieces of sunshine pop.'

Despite all the adulation, there were still reservations.

'The problem is that Ocean Colour Scene are a wonderful Hall of Mirrors reflection of Brit guitar pop's most recent obsessions, but their music appears to be devoid of any personal quirk, twist, deviancy or strangeness that comes directly from the four people in the band. It's all too efficient, it's all too beautiful. It's all too vaudeville.

Where OCS do distinguish themselves from the pack of 60s updates is in Simon's unabashed determination to act the prettiest star. All pouting lips (McCulloch), fluttering eyeshadowed lids (Bowie) and stilted moves (Jagger), Simon gives a kind of flicker-book impersonation of Rock Star Androgynous Narcissism throughout the ages.

'During Fly Me, Simon tries unsuccessfully to levitate from the stage by flapping his arms like a lead goose. This is not a good moment. Then, during Sway, he points Ziggy-ishly at lucky people in the crowd, some of whom, mostly older and male, are already taking the piss out of his theatrics. A lot of the girls, though, are singing along, and looking kind of entranced.

'It's not that Simon's impersonation of a pop god is that bad. The ocean will part for the band. But it does make it all the harder for OCS to convince that they have much that is mysterious or ingenious to contribute in their own right.'

(Years later, Simon said to Mojo magazine: 'I probably deserved the criticism. I was a bit of a twat. I was on a Mick Jagger trip.')

Simon's slightly too enthusiastic on-stage performance was probably due to the fact that, the very next day, the band were due to begin recording their debut album with legendary American producer Jimmy Miller, who had more or less come out of retirement on their behalf. Miller was revered by Simon and Cradock in particular for his work on Rolling Stones' albums such as Let It Bleed, Sticky Fingers, Beggars Banquet and Goat's Head Soup. Originally, he was to share production duties with hip dance producer Steve Osbourne, fresh from a huge success with the Happy Mondays. It should have been the perfect fusion of 60s and 90s.

At the time, Simon admitted to NME: 'I know people will say we got in Jimmy Miller because we wanted to sound like The Stones. But what actually happened was that he was invited to one of our gigs, we met and all got on really well. Just after Christmas, we heard he wanted to work on the album. We thought we'd try him out. He hasn't got a bad track record, has he?'

Ocean Colour Scene later claimed that Jimmy Miller taught them about being in a band. His heavy

drinking, however, didn't do the recording process much good. As Simon later said to Q: 'Jimmy opened the door to a big party.'

The group spent more time getting stoned and downing bottles of Jack Daniels than working on their songs, despite the fact that they were stupidly spending their future earnings on studios such as Marcus, Townhouse, Greenhouse and Eden, some of which cost up to £1,000 per day.

'But as a youth,' Cradock recalled to Q, 'if you're going to get offered free beers all day, you'll go down that track. Fuckin' right you will. But the vibe from those sessions was there. We just needed to sober up and get a few straight vocals down and it was in the bag.'

Summer turned into autumn and Jimmy Miller found himself out of a job. Fontana insisted that a replacement be brought in and the album re-recorded all over again. Ocean Colour Scene didn't want to lose Jimmy, but could understand why the record company was anxious about the outcome.

The first new producer drafted in was Hugo Nicholson, who was chosen because of his engineering and co-production work on Primal Scream's recent, highly acclaimed indie-dance album Screamadelica. However, Dave Bates, Fontana's head of A&R, who had previously signed bands such as Big Country and Def Leppard, still wasn't happy.

'The tapes just didn't sound as good as the band did live,' Bates told Q years later. 'They just didn't carry the same strength.'

'Dave Bates had this idea that all the bands on the label should sound the same,' was Simon's conclusion in a Time Out interview. 'He'd play us stuff by The Catherine Wheel and The House of Love, where he had assumed an executive-producer role. And the producers who were working on those albums would meet in order to try to make it sound the same, because he had this notion that the Bates Empire would become like an English Motown.'

The re-recording did have one advantage, though. At one stage, sessions moved to Paul Weller's Solid Bond studios at London's Marble Arch, where Ocean Colour Scene met both Weller and Brendan Lynch for the first time. Brendan Lynch, now Paul Weller's producer, was then an engineer at his studio. He was also in the process of working on the Young Disciples' only album, Road

Is it two years too late for Solihull's swooningly psychedelic four-piece?

'Is it two years too late for Solihull's swooningly psychedelic four-piece?'

because **Paul Weller** was in it and he's huge over

e, and he talked about us interviews

To Freedom, which became a soulful influence on all of the band.

'Paul had bought Sway and Yesterday Today and was really into us,' Damon told Record Collector. 'He heard we were in the studio and came down to meet us. We got on like a house on fire. We did a few gigs with him during that time.'

Forced to begin recording their own album for the third time, the band were beginning to grow bored with the songs, some of which they had already been playing live for almost two years. This time around, their designated producer was to be Tim Palmer, famous for his work with heavy-handed rock acts such as Pearl Jam. If the relationship with Fontana was already very strained, it quickly grew worse when their former single, Sway, was suddenly re-released in February against the group's wishes. Worse still, it peaked at an embarrassingly mediocre No 88 - much lower than it had first time around on an indie label. Just one month later, another single, Giving It All Away, limped into the charts at No 83. With public interest in the band rapidly evaporating, despite their initial promise, the release of their eponymously titled debut album in April was all but ignored.

'Is it two years too late for Solihull's swooningly psychedelic four-piece?' asked Vox. 'Ocean Colour Scene billow melodically from the same sun-dappled 60s hinterland as a hundred other bands, but prefer to hint at pastel-shaded pastiche rather than out-and-out crass parody. Their depth and quaintness suggested they'd outlive the baggy scene - as well as those thuggish contemporaries who mocked their subtle melodic fare - and this first album's long gestation period has allowed them to refine their spaced-out sparkle and surging harmonies into quietly magnificent space.

'Despite the ersatz West Coast twang to Simon Fowler's vulnerable whine, this is a band undeniably more adept at the fragile whimsy of Syd Barrett-era Brit trippiness than its duly anti-social American cousins. Hence the breezy summer storm of Giving It All Away and the acoustic sob of Justine sound far less forced than street-funk snorters like Do Yourself a Favour or the strung-out, Stonesey drawl of Three Shades of Green.'

The truth was that the album was simply too long in the making and, in the end, it was just not good enough. An association with the baggy scene was no longer all that was required to break it big. Ironically, however, some reviewers did notice the new direction that the band were trying to take.

'Emerging from Solihull just moments before the baggy bubble burst,' mused NME, 'Ocean Colour Scene were rapidly derided when it became apparent that they had missed the bus. What this debut LP proves beyond doubt is that Ocean Colour Scene didn't miss the last bus to Madchester - they were never even trying to catch it. Their 18-month hiatus - broken only by the worrying release of singles persistently snubbed by record buyers - has arguably benefited Ocean Colour Scene. The inclusion of Sway on the album serves only to highlight just how far the Scene have developed, from bemused owners of a wah-wah pedal to excitable custodians of a bulging bag of pick'n'mix pop goodies.

'It is perhaps no coincidence that Hugo

'For 11 months, we couldn't even play

"Screamadelica" Nicholson enjoys several production credits, or that the legendary Stones knob-twiddler, Jimmy Miller, was also calling the shots over some tracks. Like Screamadelica, Ocean Colour Scene is a great mess of snatched styles, a patchwork that can only be the work of someone passionately besotted by pop and its fabbest icons.

'Apart from the funk work-out of Stevie Wonder's Do Yourself a Favour, the remaining 11 tracks are, to varying degrees, sparkling moments of pure pop that establish Ocean Colour Scene as first-class graduates from the Real Song School. Justine, a delicate, acoustic number, swelled by deep, mourning cellos, is as far away from the languid, psychedelic swirl of the opener, Talk On, as it is possible to get on one record, probably. Surging guitars and intricate harmonies permeate the whole LP, most successfully on the Lennon-esque One of these Days, while Third Shade of Green is magnificent. Gently stirring in that ambient, Stonesy fashion that Bobby Gillespie is so adept at, the song is gradually swamped by wave upon wave of swelling guitars. An admirable continuation of the lineage.'

This was perhaps an overly kind review of Ocean Colour Scene's debut album. Certainly, the seeds of great songs and fine musicianship were apparent, but the band were capable of producing a much better album, and they knew it.

'By the end,' Simon confessed to Q magazine, 'there wasn't the feeling there. We'd been exposed to too much of the music business. We were doing drugs and going to clubs. That's where our highs were. They weren't in the music.'

Despite many promising aspects to several songs, the LP was clearly badly blurred by overproduction. (Bizarrely, it also featured Alison Moyet on backing vocals.) Only two tracks were left over from the Jimmy Miller sessions - Penny Pinching Rainy Heaven Days (which Simon now calls his favourite track from that time) and Justine.

'The last time we listened to that album,' Simon told Q, 'it sounded really bizarre, like it was sponsored by some reverb company.'

Meanwhile, matters continued to go from bad to awful.

In May 1992, a third single was released by Fontana. It was a cover of Stevie Wonder and Syreeta Wright's Do Yourself a Favour. It made for their worst chart placing yet, at No 94.

Already out of favour in Britain, Ocean Colour Scene made an attempt to sell themselves abroad. First, they went to Japan.

'We had a great time there,' Damon told Record Collector, 'because Paul Weller was into us and he's huge over there, and he talked about us in interviews. Our promoter phoned up and asked us to go over there. We made a profit of £20,000 from playing five gigs. We were really popular there, like being in The Beatles.'

Then Fontana tried to break the band in the States by sending them on a North American tour as part of a record-company package, alongside label-mates The House of Love and Catherine Wheel.

'It was brilliant,' Simon told Q. 'Seven weeks, 28 cities, 12,000 miles. We did a good gig at the Academy in New York and went down really well. But we did a gig in New Orleans in a 1,400-capacity

couldn't record, we gig in our local pub.

shed and there were only 10 people there - and eight of them were on our coach.'

Steve recalls exactly the same date in New Orleans - but not because of the number of people at the gig.

'We were in New Orleans, stoned out of our heads,' he recalled to Arena. 'This old woman came up to me and told me she would read my fortune. So she leads me into this tiny, pitch-black room and starts throwing these chicken stones across the floor and telling me that I was 23, in a band, and that I was destined to be really successful.'

The woman may have been able to see years into the future, but she didn't notice what was just around the corner. By the time the band got to Boston, Fowler had to be admitted to hospital to be treated for exhaustion.

'It was a combination of homesickness and staying up late,' Simon said to Time Out. 'My entire body was revolting against me. I was in a big waiting room with all these mad people and down-and-outs, then two hours later I was back at the venue. When I returned, the rest of the band were working out an instrumental version of the set. It was like Nigel Tufnell returning to Spinal Tap.'

Subsequently, and with the Americans hardly eager to snap up Ocean Colour Scene singles, the tour began to disintegrate.

'We knew it at the time,' Steve later told Q. 'We knew we'd fucked Bates off and we knew we'd had it.'

By the end of 1992, Ocean Colour Scene were back in Birmingham and ready to begin work on their follow-up album. Their plan was to get the LP recorded as quickly as possible, then return to the States to tour. They completed the demos in a matter of weeks, but when they gave the tape to the record company, the reaction was not what they had hoped for.

'We gave the demos to Fontana, but they hated them,' Damon told Record Collector. 'After a couple of months, we just decided, that's it then. There was a tune called Magical, one called Hello Monday and another called It's a Beautiful Thing, which were killers.'

'We intended to finish off a few new songs to record the next album,' Simon told Record Collector. 'But Dave Bates - the dickhead at Fontana - said no.'

In Q magazine years later, while talking about that period, Steve became visibly upset.

'I remember Bates being on his knees,' he recalled. 'He was saying, "I don't think you understand how to write singles," and we never once said we could write singles. No group goes up to someone and says, "We've got four smash singles here." Groups don't fuckin' know.

'He was saying, "You're too whimsical. You sound like fuckin' Simon & Garfunkel." So we were like, "You've got a fuckin' little Scalextrix set in your office, you cunt, how can we take you seriously?" He wanted to be Andrew Loog Oldham in a way. He used to get the producers round his house for a morning swim in the nude and then they'd sit down and play records together and decide how they wanted their groups to sound.'

Q then asked Bates whether or not this accusation was true.

'Steve is full of shit,' he replied. 'I think that's a bit of fertile imagination. Skinny-dipping with producers first thing in the morning? Interesting turn of phrase, but not true.'

Needless to say, the split was far from amicable. Ocean Colour Scene spent almost a year trying to get out of their contract with Fontana. Steve's dad, Chris Cradock, the band's long-term manager, sacked the lawyer that had been provided by Phonogram and employed his own, Michael Thomas, who was also the lawyer of Peter Gabriel.

'He hated Dave Bates and happened to come and see one of our gigs by accident,' Damon told Record Collector. 'We met him and were telling him our troubles. He said, "Right, I'm going to get you out of the deal." He did it all for free because we couldn't afford a lawyer at this point. We were broke, basically. He was like a godsend.

'For 11 months, we couldn't record, we couldn't even play a gig in our local pub. It was all because the contract we had was so terrible. Ultimately, that was why we were able to walk out of the deal. It was ridiculous. We owed them half a million pounds, so they certainly wanted us to stay, but we walked.'

My entire body was revolting against me. I was in a big waiting room with all these mad people and down-and-outs

"My entire body was reacting against me. I was in a big waiting room with all these mad people, down and outs.

down
mad and outs

Chapter Three

By 1993, Ocean Colour Scene were back on the dole and as far away from pop stardom as they had been since they were in their first bands at school. The optimism instilled in them by the Stone Roses had all but vanished, there was no sign of any of the money they were supposed to have earned and nobody seemed to be the slightest bit interested in their music any more. Q magazine later revealed that, during this lean period, Steve's dad, Chris Cradock, was forced to arrange a second mortgage on his house to raise finances and, after a property slump in the area, he put the family home up for sale.

As for the band, they had not given up hope. They were writing and recording new songs, biding their time before, they assumed, another major label would realise their talent and snap them up.

'Even when we left Fontana,' Steve later told Q, 'and we were just working on the 8-track, we still thought we were making an album. We were getting all psychedelic, stoned off our boxes, and imagining we were making some fucked up 8-track underground album. That's what used to get us through.'

Chris Cradock discussed this grim time with Q.

'I think if we're to be really, really honest about it,' he told Tom Doyle, 'we all had the odd bad day, though we never ever had it on the same day. I can remember one occasion where Steve was away somewhere and he phoned me and I was really down, and that night there was a knock on the front door and it was the other three band members. Basically they'd come to cheer me up. It was the same when Simon had a few bad days. We picked him up. Everyone was the same. Never once did they lose that belief.'

'I remember when Steve first joined Paul Weller's band,' Simon recalled to NME. 'I'd be sitting at home on the dole in this fuckin' freezing-cold house writing songs and he'd be off playing gigs all around the world. And him doing that was the only good thing in my life, and it really was fantastic. Because I knew that however bad things were for me, Steve was still having a good time, and that no matter what, one day we'd get the band back together.'

Chris Cradock (who was responsible for setting up offices for Ocean Colour Scene in Birmingham's Custard Factory arts complex) also spoke to Select about the determination of his son's group.

'I'm an ex-copper, right,' he told the magazine. '25 years in the police force. And I have never, ever known four characters with the guts and determination of these lads. I've never come across it before, in any walk of life.'

Perhaps Ocean Colour Scene would eventually have given up on their belief that they were born to be rock'n'roll stars. Before they had the chance, however, help came along in the form of their old friend - and still one of their principal musical heroes - Paul Weller.

In March 1993 Weller, still out of favour himself, asked the band to support him at a gig at the Town & Country Club in Leeds. It was the confidence boost the band needed. Their show also made Paul Weller realise how good a guitar player Steve Cradock really was. Paul was just finding his musical feet again, and was in the process of writing the song - called The Weaver - that was to signal his own rebirth. He asked Steve if he would like to play guitar on the song, even though it had not yet been chosen by his own record company, Go! Discs, to be released as a single.

'Paul played me this acetate of The Weaver in the garden at Solid Bond,' Steve recalled to Record Collector. 'I was like, "Where can I buy it from?" Wicked! It was a real education for me. It totally turned around my playing. A lot of the real precious moments I've got are just sitting around when Paul's playing the guitar - it's almost spiritual sometimes. A confidence-booster? I don't know. I was always aware that I was good. We couldn't get a gig in any shithole in England. Nobody would touch us. But it never did get in the way - it's just that our time wasn't right.'

It wasn't just Steve who was lifted by Paul Weller's attention, though. It was the entire band.

'I think maybe at first we were kind of thinking that not having a record deal would be a fairly temporary thing,' Simon told Q. 'Then Steve started playing with Paul and that just illuminated everything. That was when everything started to get exciting again.'

The Weller-Cradock relationship went from strength to strength, particularly as Paul's career was suddenly going incredibly well. Like Ocean Colour Scene, he had been struggling to get out of a lean period. Now, he was scoring his first hit singles (although they were still far from Top 10 successes) since the 80s and the media was taking an interest in him again. He was experiencing everything that Ocean Colour Scene wanted to believe was possible for them. Coincidentally - and quite importantly for Steve - Paul had been managed since the beginning of The Jam by his father.

'Me and my dad used to be at loggerheads all the time because he wanted me to concentrate on my schoolwork and I wanted to play guitar,' Steve later confessed to NME. 'But we still stuck together. We even used to do a window-cleaning round together, you know. We were always trying to get things together. Then he started managing us and everything was fine. And that's very similar to Paul Weller, you know. There are a lot of parallels. Like

Because I knew that however **bad** things were for me, Steve was still having a good time, and that no matter what, one day we'd get the band **back together**

aying with Paul, I knew my playing was getting better. I'd

'When I was playing with **Paul**, I knew my playing was getting better. I'd had Otis Redding and B

Beatles and Booker T. albums when I was 13. I could listen to it, dig it, but I couldn't play it. That started to change,

Beatles and Booker T. albums when I was 13. I could listen to it, dig it, but I co

Paul Weller's mum's maiden name is Cradock as well. It's pretty heavy.'

On top of that, the personal boost and professional encouragement that Steve got from being asked to play with Paul Weller, and the association with the former Jam man's own rebirth would do Ocean Colour Scene no harm either.

'When I was playing with Paul,' Cradock told Q, 'I knew my playing was getting better. I'd had Otis Redding and Booker T albums when I was 13. I could listen to it, dig it, but I couldn't play it. That started to change.'

During the summer and autumn of 1993, Steve took a temporary sabbatical from Ocean Colour Scene to concentrate on his apprenticeship with Weller, who was recording his second solo album, the highly acclaimed Wild Wood at The Manor in Oxfordshire. Not only did the pair get on incredibly well both musically and personally, but Steve also managed to persuade Paul that he should bring in Simon Fowler to help out on backing vocals. The album, of course, spawned several Top 10 singles, reached No 2 in the charts and went on to sell 1,000,000 copies. The result was a demand for Paul Weller to tour Britain almost non-stop. He asked Steve to join him. At some gigs, even Simon was on stage to sing an acoustic set as support.

Steve admitted to Q that it was nerve-wracking playing with someone as talented and inspirational as Weller.

'Maybe at the start I got a bit too nervous and began acting like too much of a fan,' he confessed. 'But eventually I just chilled out. I kept thinking about things like on the back of the last Jam album, Dig the New Breed, where he signed off with Belief Is All - things like that really kept me going when I was a kid. Now I've had him doing things he maybe wouldn't have done, like playing Tales from the Riverbank. I even got him to play Going Underground for me backstage one night when he was pissed, and he'd never do that live. In a way, I'm maybe the best thing that came out of that Belief Is All thing.'

Steve spent the following six months touring throughout the world with Paul Weller, learning what it was like to be part of a truly successful and professional outfit. He ploughed as much of the money as possible back into Ocean Colour Scene.

In March 1994, Paul Weller asked both Simon and Steve to attend recording sessions for a new song. It was called Hung Up and it was to become Weller's first Top 10 hit for years. In support of the single, Weller headed out on yet another UK tour, this time not only with Steve on guitar, but with Simon on backing vocals. Simon even used to come on stage on his own at the end of Weller's set to perform a stunning cover of Erma Franklin's soul classic Another Little Piece of my Heart. Journalists at Weller's gigs suddenly began to take an interest

in the singer. Perhaps the band weren't over after all. Things were looking up for Ocean Colour Scene.

The band knew, however, that they would have to capitalise on the exposure they had received through their association with Paul Weller. Nobody was going to hand them another record deal. But the 60s-influenced music they were making was starting to get fashionable again, so they knew that it was now or never.

Chris Cradock began organising a few low-key London dates for the band, inviting record company executives along and hoping to cash in on the first optimistic signs that Ocean Colour Scene had experienced in years.

The first person in a position of power to register his interest was Andy McDonald, the head of independent label Go! Discs, also home to Paul Weller.

'Andy McDonald gave Steve a Christmas present of sixteen grand's worth of recording gear,' Damon admitted to Record Collector. 'We were also given £5,000 by Go! Discs because, through Paul and Steve, Andy was really into us and wanted to hear some demos. He wanted to sign us but he had no time to fit us in on his roster.'

One of the gigs that Ocean Colour Scene played while trying to attract record-company funding was at the Splash Club in London's King's Cross in April 1994. By this time, Paul Weller was being hailed as one of Britain's best male recording artists. Thus it didn't go unnoticed when he turned up at his friends' gig and even got up on stage to guest with them. Subsequently, journalists even started turning up at every Ocean Colour Scene concert in the hope that they would catch a rare, impromptu Paul Weller performance.

There appeared to be only one thing stopping Ocean Colour Scene from being signed up by a major record label for the second time - their name. All the labels wanted to present the band to the public as a brand-new proposition. The group, however, wouldn't budge on that issue. They felt they had been through so much all by themselves, relying on their own belief, that they weren't going to give in on anything now.

Asked by Record Collector's John Reed why they didn't change their name, Steve said simply, 'But it's a wicked name, innit?'

'There's this thing about our name,' he continued. 'When nobody would sign us and we were doing gigs in shitholes, all the record companies and publishers turned around and said, no, that name, it's so unfashionable. We were like, you can't say that. You don't realise how good it is.'

'The main crux of the problem was definitely the name,' Steve's dad, Chris Cradock, told Q. 'I remember going to Virgin and this A&R woman said, "Before I play any tracks, are the band prepared to change their name?" And I said, "No,

d said, no, that **name**, it's so unfashionable. We we
me, that **name**, it's so unfashionable. We were.
shionable. We were

I kept thinking about things like on the back of the last Jam album, D

Belief Is All

-things like that really kept

they won't." She said, "Well, in that case, there's the door." '

'Towards the end,' Steve told Q in the same interview, 'we told Chris that if they were giving him any shit about the name, just to tell them to fuck off and put the phone down. He started doing that and about a month later we were getting a vibe going.'

By the spring of 1994, however, even an unfashionable name and short-sighted record-company executives couldn't put a hold on the momentum that Ocean Colour Scene's revitalised career was gathering. Although Steve was still away on tour with Paul Weller in Europe and the States, progress was being made. Simon was busy writing a brand-new batch of songs on the equipment donated to the band by Andy McDonald. He was inspired by the industry's sudden interest in retro British guitar bands, too. Despite the fact that Steve could easily have made a very good living by becoming part of Weller's touring band full time, it was only a temporary measure until Ocean Colour Scene were back in action themselves.

In June of 1994, the Weller touring party returned to Britain to headline Saturday night at the Glastonbury festival. Playing their first Glastonbury appearance the following afternoon were Oasis. Oasis were already at the forefront of the new wave of Britpop, although to date they had only put out two relatively successful singles. Both Liam and Noel Gallagher turned up at Glastonbury a day early, principally to watch Weller's set. The pair had already met Ocean Colour Scene at several gigs and industry events. The first time they chatted was when Oasis were on their second UK club tour and they played at Ocean Colour Scene's local venue, the Jug of Ale. Noel was very impressed by Cradock in particular over the Glastonbury weekend. Later, when Noel was given a tape of Ocean Colour Scene's new demos, he decided to ask them to support Oasis on their Live Forever tour that August.

'When you had your shoe-gazing and your Kurt Cobain,' Steve later reasoned in Q, 'we realised that nothing was going to happen for us because people were growing their hair and getting angry and moody. Then when Oasis came along, we just thought that something was kicking off again. People remembered that there was something happening with the baggy thing and it was a lot better for everyone than Nirvana. As soon as we saw Oasis, we knew the vibe was back. And they saw something happening for us at a time when everyone was telling us that we were hanging out of our arses and that we'd lost it. I respect them for that.'

With Oasis rapidly becoming the hottest new British band for more than a decade, the support

slot was the ultimate sign that Ocean Colour Scene were about to make it big.

For several months in autumn 1994, Paul Weller went back out on tour with Steve in tow. This time, however, he also asked Ocean Colour Scene bassist Damon Minchella to join them.

'I became much better over that six months,' Damon confessed to Record Collector. 'I had to. I was playing bass with the best drummer in the world, Steve White. Simon did the Wild Wood tour, too, and most of the Stanley Road tour. He came out with us all over the world and played a lot of the tunes from our album, Moseley Shoals. He also did a storming version of Live Forever. Oscar came out on the English tour, playing piano with Simon, so Ocean Colour Scene took over Paul's bus.'

Paul Weller's next single, Out of the Sinking, featured all four members of the band for the first time. Steve was on guitar, Damon was playing bass on the b-side cover of The Beatles' Sexy Sadie, Oscar played piano and Simon sang backing vocals.

There could be no stopping the Birmingham band achieving their long-held ambitions now. At the tail end of 1994, Ocean Colour Scene signed a publishing deal with Island Music, after they had passed a demo to the label's Nigel Coxon.

'Nigel came to see us,' Damon told Record Collector, 'then gave us a publishing deal the next day, which basically saved our necks.'

With the money from Island, Ocean Colour Scene set up their own studio just outside Birmingham. They decided to christen it Moseley Shoals.

'The studio isn't actually in Moseley [an area of Birmingham],' Damon revealed to Record Collector. 'It's in an area called Five Ways. But Five Ways Shoals didn't really fit in. I'm from Liverpool originally, but we all live around Moseley. It's nearer the centre of Birmingham, whereas Solihull is a posh, southern part. Our studio is in a very industrial area. It's where Dexy's Midnight Runners recorded their first album.'

With their own studio up and running, Ocean Colour Scene set to work straight away to record as many of their own songs as possible. By now it was no longer a question of whether or not a record company would sign them, but rather which they would choose to go with.

In the end, it was MCA - as one of Nigel Coxon's good friends turned out to be an A&R man for that label. On a tip from Coxon, he travelled up to Birmingham to visit Ocean Colour Scene in their studio and listen to their new songs. He offered to sign them immediately. The band were on their way to their second deal with a major record company - only this time, they were determined to do things the best way. Their own way.

Then when Oasis came along, we just thought that something was kicking off again. People remember

was something happening with the baggy thing and it was a lot better for everyone than **Nirvana.**

Chapter Four

Two days into 1995, **Ocean Colour Scene** began work on what was - finally - to be the follow-up to their debut album.

'On that first day in the studio,' Damon told Record Collector, 'we recorded demos of Lining Your Pockets and The Downstream, along with Fairport Convention's Meet on the Edge and Mr Bojangles, for some reason. We'd just got the gear in and we were trying it out, but those first two tunes, with a couple of overdubs, ended up on the album. The whole thing was written and recorded in the space of eight weeks. It was so quick because most of it was live takes, with a few overdubs and mixing.'

Although the band knew that they were working on something special (not to mention something which that would certainly fit in nicely with the new mood in Britain for retro rock boosted by the massive, international success of Oasis), both Steve and Damon continued to record and play with Paul Weller during this period. In part, it was because the exposure and experience would benefit Ocean Colour Scene in the future. It was also because the band had chosen Brendan Lynch as their producer - he had worked with Paul Weller and was tied up for a lot of the time on Weller's new album, Stanley Road. The band had chosen him because he loved old, analogue equipment and was the best choice to recreate the early 70s sound that they were after. He also shared their passion for The Beatles and old soul music. To secure his services, they were prepared to wait.

Ocean Colour Scene, however, did play one gig of their own during the recording of Moseley Shoals. It was in early summer at a club called the Blue Note in London. Paul Weller's biographer Paolo Hewitt had written a Small Faces book and was in the process of putting together a tribute album to the band, to which Ocean Colour Scene had agreed to contribute. They performed a short set of their new songs, accompanied by singer PP Arnold. Perhaps for the first time, the record-industry people present began to wonder if they shouldn't have signed the group themselves.

Ocean Colour Scene's first radio performance of their new material also came courtesy of Paolo Hewitt. He was responsible for securing them a slot on a GLR radio programme he was hosting with Paul Weller, even though their debut single was not scheduled to be released for at least another six months. By now, the band were playing regular small club gigs. When they appeared at London's infamous 100 club, Noel Gallagher was with them on stage. Naturally, press interest increased considerably.

As a final boost to the band's credibility and yet another pointer towards how much they had improved during their four-year sabbatical out of the public eye, Simon Fowler was recruited as support on Paul Weller's final, autumn tour of 1995. He played harmonica and had his own solo acoustic spot. It was at the same time that MCA decided to test the waters for the band. They mailed out several hundred promotional copies of the group's song You Got It Bad to radio stations and selected journalists. The result was some promising air play and positive reviews. Finally, it seemed, people were beginning to forget - or at least willing to forgive - Ocean Colour Scene's disastrous baggy-period debut.

The song sounds like Spender Davis Group's Keep on Running pla

free at a northern soul party

They want something that is a bit lasting, not just some transi

ng they can forget about the next day.

'It was just a few hundred white-label copies of the song that came out in November to create a bit of a buzz,' Damon explained to Record Collector. 'We didn't want to put out a single cold. We wanted something that we knew people would dig. It got A-listed on Greater London Radio.'

Everything was going so well that - if they considered their past form with regard to good luck - Ocean Colour Scene should have been anticipating a disaster. On New Year's Day 1996, just as they were preparing to put out their first single in almost five years, their Moseley Shoals studio in Birmingham flooded, ruining most of their equipment. The band, of course, had come through worse disasters than this and - to their credit - they decided not to let it put them off. They began rebuilding work immediately, having already decided to double the studio's size. The songs for the album, thankfully, were already complete. Plans to release The Riverboat Song as their first single in February remained unchanged.

At this stage a new, influential fan muscled in on the picture. BBC Radio 1 DJ Chris Evans - whose breakfast show on the station was then pulling in about four million listeners every morning - adored the song. He made it his single of the week and asked the band to appear on the first-ever show of his new Channel 4 series, TFI Friday. They turned up to perform The Riverboat Song, only to be asked if the show could use snippets from the song throughout the entire programme. The band, of course, agreed. The riff chosen by the show's producers proved so popular that by the next week, they had decided to use it as the theme music to the whole series. With all this credible publicity and their excellent batch of new material, Ocean Colour Scene simply couldn't fail.

In its first week in the shops, The Riverboat Song sold several thousand copies. It entered the charts just inside the Top 10. It was to remain in the upper reaches of the Top 40 for more than a month.

'We feel vindicated big time,' Damon told Q. 'We couldn't get a gig outside of a shithole three months ago. We stuck at it 'cos we love it. And we've still got things to prove.'

Record Collector later described The Riverboat Song as 'late 60s/early 70s riff rock, with a touch of driving organ courtesy of Paul Weller'. The magazine also noted that 'Oasis, Weller and Ocean Colour Scene mine the same rock seam - roughly that of 1966-71'.

'Earnest, melodic guitar rock is back in fashion,' they rightly stated. For Ocean Colour Scene, they also correctly observed that one had to 'add in the blues of early 70s bands - the ones that punk set out to destroy - like Thin Lizzy, Joe Cocker and Free'. It was to be this final sentiment that would plague the band throughout their imminent success, particularly from the press.

Damon confessed to Record Collector that The Riverboat Song came from Free and Peter Green's Fleetwood Mac.

Talking to Record Collector about writing the track, Damon said: 'We were sitting there having a jam around a 12-bar riff. And it turned out to be a record that sold 60,00 copies. They played it on Sportsnight sometimes, when they showed the highlights of the matches. It has been a nice money-spinner, I have to say.'

At the end of the following month, Ocean Colour Scene put out their second new single. Entitled You've Got It Bad, the track was described

Ocean Colour Scene unashamed

mine a seam left unattended since prog arrived: tuff-soul, British R&B, school of Winwood, Stewart and Marriott.

Earnest, melodic guitar rock is back

fashion

I mean real heritage: top the fuckin' **Beatles** and I'll knock you out. Nobody did it better than **The Beatles.**

by Record Collector as 'the first true mod record of our time'. They added: 'The song sounds like Spender Davis Group's Keep on Running played by Free at a northern soul party'. More simply, Damon described the song to the magazine as 'a two-chord northern soul stomp, but modern-sounding'. You've Got It Bad mimicked The Riverboat Song's commercial success by entering the charts within the Top 10. Everything was set for the release of Moseley Shoals, the band's second album, named - naturally - after their own studio.

Moseley Shoals finally came out in April 1996 and entered the UK album charts at No 2. Nobody - not even the band themselves - could have guessed how long it would remain in the Top 10. Before its release, Q magazine described the LP as 'quite the most accomplished record to be turned in by a British group this year'.

'Our sound totally dates back to the Jimmy Miller sessions,' Steve confessed to the magazine in the same interview. 'I was thinking the other day how much I wish he was still alive, 'cos he'd fuckin' love what we're doing now. That's when it was defined.'

Of Moseley Shoals, Mojo's Jim Irvin said: 'Ocean Colour Scene unashamedly mine a seam left unattended since prog arrived: tuff-soul, British R&B, school of Winwood, Stewart and Marriott.'

Asked by Record Collector what inspired him as a songwriter, Simon, then 31, replied: 'I left my parents home quite late, when I was 26. I moved to Moseley and bang, life started. That is reflected on Moseley Shoals. This title is a joke, really. It's about experiences, highs and lows and all the bits inbetween. So I write about myself and my friends. Lyrically, the singles have lyrics that I'm more emotionally divorced from. They're just wordplay.'

He did admit to NME, however, that he could not have produced a second album as good as Moseley Shoals if it had come out directly after their debut.

'We could never have made an album like Moseley Shoals without the wait,' he said. 'If everything had gone right for us first time around, I really don't think we'd still be around now. We would have made an album, it would have got to No 37 or something and then we would have been crushed by the pressure of the industry. The fact is that all this time preparing to make a second album has meant that it has got that mood of sadness to it, while still being positive. Having been in the doldrums just means I can write better songs for having been there. It's like So Sad About Us or Disguises by The Who. There's a form of despair in those songs but they both still manage to convey this optimism through it. That's exactly what we're trying to do.'

Not everyone was so enthusiastic, though. Like several publications, monthly magazine Vox, which

'We were sitting there having a jam around a 12-bar riff. And it turned out to be a record that sold **60,00 copies.** They played it on Sportsnight sometimes, when they showed the highlights of the matches. It has been a nice money-spinner.'

awarded the album only three out of 10, blazed with accusations of retro posturing.

'Like owning a wardrobe full of Sta-prest trousers in 1996, Ocean Colour Scene records beg the question, "Why?" ' declared the album's reviewer. 'The Riverboat Song was as smart as a vintage-tailored jacket, while Simon Fowler's voice was a hybrid of several white 80s R&B chappies more famous than he'll ever be. But jazz. In Modville, myriad bands have taken that riff better, worn cooler shades, and delivered a far better-defined agenda.

'It's only four years since their debut album, but Ocean Colour Scene are 20 years older. 40 Past Midnight, a tambourine-abusing, smoky, bar-guitar rankle, makes them sound like they would have been third on the bill to Jethro Tull in 1974. You've Got It Bad mirrors the overall catchiness of The Riverboat Song, but as far as highlights go, that's your lot. The sluggish One for the Road is nearer the bum-fluff mark. Cast sound like Tricky by comparison. Ocean Colour Scene would be much better off running a clothes shop in Carnaby Street.'

Of course, by now, such criticism barely mattered, although it angered the band themselves.

'It's fuckin' absurd that we even have to answer accusations that we're retro because it's bringing an agenda to it that's irrelevant,' Simon fumed in Time Out. 'To me, it's folk music. And by that I don't mean lots of minstrels with lutes dancing around a maypole. I mean real heritage: top the fuckin' Beatles and I'll knock you out. Nobody did it better than The Beatles.'

Both Simon and Steve kept the debate about their old-fashioned musical tendencies going in interviews with the press throughout the summer.

'We play the sort of music I like,' Simon told Sky. 'I mean, of course it's retro, the nature of pop music itself is retro. Techno is just Kraftwerk from 1974, know what I mean? Anyway, how can I know anything about young people's music? I'm 31.'

'What people are appreciating again is the mood of the song, no matter when it was released,' Simon was quoted in NME as saying. 'There's this idea that anything that was released before Anarchy in the UK is just old-fashioned, that taking an influence from before then is retrogressive. That's just bollocks. There was a lot of coffee-table cocaine rock around that time, 1975, especially coming out of LA. All those Laurel Canyon socialites making albums, but you know, there were still good things going on in the mid-70s. Bob Dylan was still releasing good records, and Ronnie Lane.'

In the same interview with NME, Steve tried to point out that young people being into old music was not a passing fad.

'What the press don't understand,' he said, 'is that a lot of people have been listening to older records in clubs for years. They have been playing them in clubs in Birmingham for ages now, and people have been getting into it. They want something that is a bit lasting, not just some transient thing they can forget about the next day. We are just out to prove all those dickheads wrong who don't understand that. I think there is a lot of people who have taken too much E and listen to music and say, "That's taking me off into space, man," and does it fuck! They just wake up the next morning and nothing has changed at all.'

Neither Steve nor Simon, however, liked the response that NME made to their comments. Later, speaking to Time Out, Simon recalled the result of the article.

'When it got to the stage where NME could no longer ignore us,' he stated, 'they put us on the cover and devoted the whole issue to whether or not we should be alive.'

Of course, he was exaggerating - but only slightly. The weekly paper had by now invented a new so-called 'musical' phrase to describe the late-60s and early-70s-influenced bands that were so popular that summer. The word they chose was 'dadrock', and it was meant to refer to dull, uninspired, boring groups of male rock musicians. Oasis, without doubt the principal protagonists, managed to escape much of the flak simply because they were so hip and important to the press. Bands like Cast - whose debut album was also in the process of selling to platinum status - copped a fair amount of criticism. It was Ocean Colour Scene, however, who came in for the most damming write-ups.

'Dadrock, right,' Steve complained to Q magazine. 'Whatever cunt came up with that can go and suck his arse. The blues, right, is an everyday emotion that is almost supposed to be caned out of you. With R&B, people will dance away their blues. People who try and say it is old-fashioned don't understand that basic release. They have to go and pay shrinks or they will end up fuckin' mad. Simon calls it folk music and I call it R&B, but we are saying the same thing, basically.'

In its first week in the shops, The Riverboat Song sold several thousand copies.

erboat Song

iverboat Song

Chapter Five

Now firmly established as the biggest 'new' band of 1996, and having proved that they were much more than one-hit wonders, **Ocean Colour Scene** took to the road full time. Contrary to what the music press were saying about them, the band's fans were not middle-aged men trying to relive their youth. They were mainly young couples or teenage boys, many of whom had been turned from fashionable dance music back on to rock'n'roll with the influence of Oasis.

It was the
however, t
band invite
friends to
tickets pr
members.
Paul We

It was the night at the Albert Hall, however, that meant the most. The band invited some of their famous friends to take part and sold tickets primarily to fan-club members. **The Real People** and **Paul Weller** were confirmed as support only the day before the concert, and **Noel Gallagher** joined the gang on the night.

Naturally, Ocean Colour Scene were still inextricably linked with the Gallaghers.

Both bands remained good friends and Ocean Colour Scene occasionally still supported Oasis, including - perhaps most memorably to date - at the two massive concerts at Manchester City's Maine Road football ground. On top of that, of course, the two groups shared a love of The Beatles and old music.

By the time Ocean Colour Scene were ready to put out another single from their platinum-selling Moseley Shoals album (in fact, it had clocked up almost 150,000 sales by the start of the summer), they had been touring non-stop for six months. At the end of their most recent tour, they played two gigs at the Electric Ballroom in Camden, north London. At the end of the concert on the second night, Noel and Liam Gallagher - who had been in the audience on both nights - got up on stage for an impromptu rendition of The Beatles' Day Tripper. From then on, it was to become Ocean Colour Scene's trademark final number.

Many critics, however, thought that Ocean Colour Scene's own new single - called The Day We Caught the Train and released in June - was almost as good as any cover they could perform. Record Collector surmised that The Day We Caught the Train 'hitched a ride with White Album-era Beatles, viewed though early-70s rock spectacles'.

Talking about the track with the band, Record Collector commented that it 'sounded very Beatles-influenced'.

To that, Simon retorted: 'I'd hope so! It wasn't intentional. No, it's more like The Who, to be honest. That line about 'You and I should ride the coast and wind up in our favourite coats miles away ... the day Jimmy caught the train', is from Quadrophenia and 5:15.'

With the song, Ocean Colour Scene also made a big leap visually. Their previous two videos had been studio-bound psychedelic affairs to suit the mood of the songs, but they were hardly inspiring. This time, the group took off to Spain with their regular video director Douglas Hart, who had previously made videos for Primal Scream, and who

also used to be bassist in the Jesus & Mary Chain. Hart filmed the four members of the band chasing around the grassy hills above the fishing port of Port Ligat in the mountainous, northeastern region of the country, which was once home to Salvador Dali.

'The bay,' reported NME, who went with the band for filming, 'hidden away from prying eyes by a headache-inducing series of winding, hillside roads, is drop-dead gorgeous. Enclosed by two uninhabited islands, the only activity here, aside from those Dali aficionados curious enough to pay homage to his house, are the fishermen who idle away their days casting nets in the pale waters of the bay. As ocean-coloured scenes go, it is perfect.'

At about the same time, the band also went to Spain to tour, as they were enjoying surprising popularity there.

'We went off to Spain because we were getting a ridiculous amount of airplay for The Riverboat Song,' Simon confessed to Record Collector. 'It was more than Michael Jackson. It was the most played record in Spain for a week - 101 plays in the first three days. So we played some gigs as a nice holiday.'

When the band returned to England, Damon and Steve returned to helping out Paul Weller - for one day only. They appeared in his band to headline a musical festival in London's Finsbury Park. Despite the fact that they were already famous - at least in terms of songs and record sales, the pair were exposed to a 34,000 strong audience for the first time ever. Incredibly, despite the band's sudden rise to pop fame, the public had been allowed to learn very little about the band members' private lives. By now, Damon and (admittedly always media-shy) drummer Oscar were all but refusing to contribute to interviews. A few people had learnt that Damon was engaged to be married, but that was about as personal as anyone had ever managed to get.

Unfortunately for Ocean Colour Scene, however, the lack of knowledge about them was taken by some to indicate that there was nothing exciting to say. Their music may have been compared endlessly to that of Oasis, but their rock'n'roll

'hitched a ride with White Album-era **Beatles**, viewed though early-70s rock spectacles'.

reputations could scarcely have been more different. While the Gallaghers continually boasted of their alcohol binges and the copious quantities of cocaine they had taken since becoming rock stars, Ocean Colour Scene stayed quiet about their extramusical activities.

'It's astonishing how little people know about us,' Steve said to Select. 'But I'll tell you something, we ain't fuckin' boring. We're full on for it. We have a mad time, all the time - we just don't want anyone to know about it.'

'I wouldn't want to be in Liam's position, in terms of his private life, which is actually very public,' Simon continued, in the same interview with Select. 'I know that sounds selfish but it's tough shit. We're not going that way. That's probably why we come across as being dull, boring fuckers in our interviews.'

As Select noted, had Ocean Colour Scene been the Stone Roses, they would have been seen as aloof, rather than uninteresting.

'The thing is,' Steve noted to the magazine, 'all we ever get asked are loads of tedious questions about our music, influences and record collections. You know, we've been asked our opinion on Spenser Davis. How exciting can you make that?'

Simon claimed the same in Sky magazine.

'People think we're boring,' he grinned, 'because in the beginning all we ever got asked was about Noel and Paul and our record company and Beatles b-sides and music, music, music. How exciting can you be about The Temptations, know what I mean?'

In August, Ocean Colour Scene were invited to support their old friends Oasis at some of the country's largest-ever gigs. First, they played two sets over two days to thousands of fans on the banks of Loch Lomond near Glasgow. Then they were part of a fuller line-up for Oasis's two gigs to 125,000 people at Knebworth. In fact, Select noted that it was the band's most recent single, The Day We Caught the Train, that visibly kick-started the event for the bulk of the audience at the first gig.

Ocean Colour Scene were not actually the first band to support Oasis and, in particular, The Chemical Brothers and the Manic Street Preachers had already stirred up some movement in the crowd. But it was that Ocean Colour Scene song that really got the thousands of retro rock fans in the audience singing.

'We walked out and I was fuckin' freaking out,' Simon explained to Select, 'but it actually gave us a real energy. After we came off, I was still just shaking. It felt like I'd been on a big dipper or something, like, "Why is the floor moving?" '

'This really is the best gig ever,' was Steve's comment to Select after he came off the stage. 'And I've probably said it far too many times already, but nobody in our time has ever seen anything like it. You want to talk about Reading festival? Forget it, man. This is one group, one event. This is fuckin' it.'

As usual, Ocean Colour Scene ended their set with a cover of Day Tripper.

'Did we tell you what happened before?' Simon asked Select. 'A couple of girls came backstage and asked us about the last time they saw us play. They asked us what the last song we played was called. It was a cover of fuckin' Day Tripper. I thought they were taking the piss, but they seriously believed we had written it.'

By Knebworth, Moseley Shoals had been in the Top 10 for six months and had sold almost half a million copies. More importantly, the album was still selling at a rate of 15,000 copies a week in the UK alone. By the end of the year, it was expected to have crossed the million mark in Britain. Ocean Colour Scene were rapidly shaping up as one of the biggest British bands of the 90s.

'The album might do a million I suppose,' Steve said to Select in the summer. 'That in itself is a bit strange because we thought it might only dip into the 30, to be honest.'

'This year has been brilliant for us,' Simon also told Select backstage at Knebworth. 'You know, we just heard we sold out the Glasgow Barrowlands in four hours, so we added an extra night. I can't wait

'It's astonishing how little people know about us, But I'll tel

But if I tell you something, we ain't fuckin' boring.

It's astonishing how little people know.

Simon, visibly moved by the whole shebang, declares, "It doesn't get much better than this, does it?"

to do it. That gig is going to be up there with playing this one to me.'

Steve was equally excitable when he got off the Knebworth stage.

'I think this whole thing has been an underground thing for the last two years and it has inspired people again,' he gushed to Select. 'It has been hotting up for a while. It has also happened at a time when nobody gives a toss about anything else. In the 80s, people were aspiring to have Porsches, weren't they? So Oasis come along and they are bigger than John Major because people believe in them. And they have far more to offer people in terms of a good time.'

A little while later, Simon talked to the NME about the extraordinary year that Ocean Colour Scene had enjoyed.

He also recalled to the paper his so-called 'lost' years working as a journalist.

'In the end, I finished up doing five years as a journalist at the Birmingham Post and the Mail,' he said, 'and sometimes I really, really regret that, because it just feels like wasted time. But what I learnt from that was that in life, anything can happen to you, no matter how unexpected. I remember the first job I ever did, I had to report on this accident where a woman had been walking along with a baby in a pram and a car had crashed into a Belisha Beacon and the top of it fell off and killed the mother outright. An absolute fluke. And I had to go and interview the driver of the car and ask him what he felt about the whole thing. I was fuckin' terrified. When you have to do something like that, you soon get your priorities in order.'

Getting their priorities in order was something that Ocean Colour Scene scarcely needed to do now, however. As anticipated, by the end of 1996, a year in which Ocean Colour Scene had played in excess of 130 live shows, Moseley Shoals had sold more than one million copies. It was the best Christmas present the band - and their families -

could have hoped for.

Ocean Colour Scene began 1997 by fulfilling yet another long-held ambition. They booked (and immediately sold out, of course) a show at London's Albert Hall. It was a venue that the band had always dreamt of playing. The concert was set for 17 February. The same week, the band sold out two further gigs at Dublin's Olympia. It was the night at the Albert Hall, however, that meant the most. The band invited some of their famous friends to take part and sold tickets primarily to fan-club members. The Real People and Paul Weller were confirmed as support only the day before the concert, and Noel Gallagher joined the gang on the night.

'Some people will never be convinced,' said NME of the gig. 'They will refuse, even after titanic nights like this, where Noel Gallagher, Paul Weller and an Albert Hall full of disciples willingly lent their assistance, to believe Ocean Colour Scene are anything but an anomaly in 1997. That their sincere devotion to the high glories of Dylan, Free and the late 60s in general - a period unplundered for years during the dreary reign of indie, remember - somehow marks them out as dullards in an age when the likes of Placebo are happily feted to the skies.

'The evening starts with Noel Gallagher sauntering onstage and happily declaring, "Welcome to the night of dad rock!" After which the Real People blitz any preconceptions of them having missed the boat and the crowd settle back in their loafers for the main event.

'There's the small matter of Paul Weller sauntering on to do a few new songs first, during which Steve Cradock, resplendent in full Noddy Holder ensemble of brown slacks and beanie cap, comes on to apply added sonic back-up for Peacock Suit, before a four-piece string ensemble turns up and performs a full, five-minute version of The Riverboat Song. At last! Evidence that the Scene have lightened up!

At least, there is a feeling that the capacity crowd at this unadvertised gig shares a secret - good music doesn't **date**

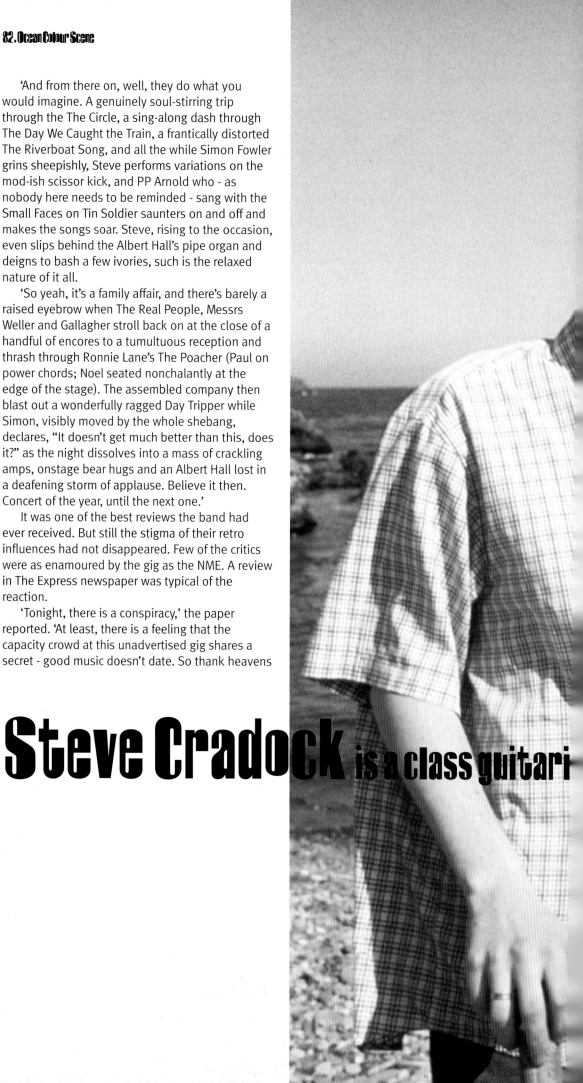

'And from there on, well, they do what you would imagine. A genuinely soul-stirring trip through the The Circle, a sing-along dash through The Day We Caught the Train, a frantically distorted The Riverboat Song, and all the while Simon Fowler grins sheepishly, Steve performs variations on the mod-ish scissor kick, and PP Arnold who - as nobody here needs to be reminded - sang with the Small Faces on Tin Soldier saunters on and off and makes the songs soar. Steve, rising to the occasion, even slips behind the Albert Hall's pipe organ and deigns to bash a few ivories, such is the relaxed nature of it all.

'So yeah, it's a family affair, and there's barely a raised eyebrow when The Real People, Messrs Weller and Gallagher stroll back on at the close of a handful of encores to a tumultuous reception and thrash through Ronnie Lane's The Poacher (Paul on power chords; Noel seated nonchalantly at the edge of the stage). The assembled company then blast out a wonderfully ragged Day Tripper while Simon, visibly moved by the whole shebang, declares, "It doesn't get much better than this, does it?" as the night dissolves into a mass of crackling amps, onstage bear hugs and an Albert Hall lost in a deafening storm of applause. Believe it then. Concert of the year, until the next one.'

It was one of the best reviews the band had ever received. But still the stigma of their retro influences had not disappeared. Few of the critics were as enamoured by the gig as the NME. A review in The Express newspaper was typical of the reaction.

'Tonight, there is a conspiracy,' the paper reported. 'At least, there is a feeling that the capacity crowd at this unadvertised gig shares a secret - good music doesn't date. So thank heavens

Steve Cradock is a class guitari

ecisely chopping and ha_ _ng around the tunes

for Ocean Colour Scene. Without them, a generation may never have known that most bands don't write songs like they used to.

'The band walk on to thunderous, if polite applause and begin on a high, blasting through singles Lining Your Pockets, The Riverboat Song and The Day We Caught the Train. As one, the audience stands, swaying along or waving their arms aloft. The group, though, seems oddly reserved. Singer Simon Fowler dances occasionally, but mostly just stands. Guitarist Steve Cradock and bassist Damon Minchella are rooted to the spot with steely concentration. So carefully crafted is each solo, the audience unconsciously finds itself appreciating the performance, rather than enjoying the gig.

'The only new song is badly received - no sing-along potential. Then the encore sees a solo acoustic performance from Fowler, followed by the inevitable stage invasion by Paul Weller, Noel Gallagher and Oasis wannabes The Real People all jamming together. They round off the evening with the obligatory Beatles cover. Day Tripper is a mess of psychedelic sounds, power chords, crescendos and crafted squall. So much talent, so little style.'

So Ocean Colour Scene continued into 1997 much as they ended 1996 - popular with the public, largely derided by the media. It is something the band need not worry about now, though. They have already begun work on the follow-up to the recently declared triple-platinum Moseley Shoals, and their popularity only appears to be on the increase. Immediately after the Albert Hall show, the band

'We went off to Spain because we were getting a ridiculous amount of airplay for The Riverboat Song. 'It was more than Michael Jackson.

That line about `You and I should ride the coast and wind up in our favourite coa[st] miles away ... the day Jimmy caught the train', is from **Quadropheni[a]**

miles away
miles away."
miles away."

confirmed that they are to headline this summer's fourth T in the Park festival in Glasgow, as well as playing tours throughout Europe, Japan and the States.

In the meantime, in March 97, the band's record company, MCA - perhaps following in the footsteps of Oasis's label, Creation - decided to put out a collection of the Ocean Colour Scene b-sides as a full-length, cut-price album. Called B-Sides, Seasides and Freerides, the album contained 14 tracks not on Moseley Shoals, including the band's by-now-familiar cover of Day Tripper, taken from the band's Electric Ballroom show in Camden last year and featuring both Noel and Liam Gallagher. There was also an acoustic version of The Day We Caught the Train.

'This collection of bonus singles tracks is a good resumé of the band at play,' said NME of the album. 'Steve Cradock is a class guitarist; precisely chopping and buzzing around the tunes. There is a threshold of playing that the band never miss, even though some of these tracks are captured in cold-water flats, during mad parties and celeb-heavy sessions.

'On Outside Of A Circle, you hear the genesis of the Moseley Shoals song The Circle. Simon Fowler rasps and someone gently picks out chords on an acoustic. The singing is less mannered here. He is not so inclined to wail and wallow, and you feel the lonely grip of the words all the more. Chicken, Bones and Stones is another song in motion, a joyous streak of Midlands soul that recalls Jim Gilstrap's Swing Your Daddy. Paul Weller plays guitar and ska legend Rico shakes a trombone. The fun in that room is practically tangible, as they all pop their fingers and wail along. Again, this is beyond Moseley Shoals in terms of the possibilities it creates.

'Many years in the wilderness, lost between baggy and Britpop, have bonded the players to an amazing degree. Thus, they can tackle the complex shape of Top of the World with its series of rhythmic swerves and mood swings. Easy. And, importantly, they don't make a big deal out of their labours. But sometimes they do act like they have aged beyond their years. Simon is constantly drawn to dismal stories - a habit that casts him as the wizened commentator. There are a million Eleanor Rigbys out there, skint, wearing musty coats, subsisting on cheap fags and painkillers. Dreams are forever slipping away as the inevitable string quartet wibbles sadly. So we will pass on Mrs Jones, Alibis and Charlie Brown Says, with their tireless sentimentality. Simon tells us on the sleeve notes that the latter song dates back to The Fanatics, his pre-Ocean Colour Scene act. Always a morbid bloke, obviously.

'Ultimately, Ocean Colour Scene need to lighten up, to enjoy the job some more. There is certainly the potential for away-day adventure on the acoustic version of The Day We Caught the Train, when Simon realises you can literally ride off the blues. It is a good song, however it is played. And you find the same liberation on Huckleberry Grove, when Shirley, the central figure, sings and dances her heart out and all the routine hassles are forgotten. For the first time ever in your career, you type out the phrase, "classic tambourine solo".'

Ocean Colour Scene are currently back in Moseley Shoals recording their third album with producer Brendan Lynch - the studio has just played host to Primal Scream, who recorded their new album there - due for release at the end of this year. Thankfully, this time, there is no question of Ocean Colour Scene disappearing for four years.

The band's epitaph to date could be summed up by a quote from singer Simon Fowler in the NME late last year.

'With Ocean Colour Scene, it has never been a question of success or failure,' he said. 'It's just the fact that the band has never stopped believing in itself, not in the entire seven years we've been together. If you stick with something you believe in, then things just happen to you, simple as that.'

can happen to you, no matter how unexpected

with **Ocean Colour Scene**, i

failure,' he said. 'It's just the fact that th

s never been a question of success or
nd has never stopped believing in itself

Discography

September 1990
Sway - single - !Phffft

March 1991
Yesterday Today - single - Fontana

February 1992
Sway - single - Fontana

March 1992
Giving It All Away - single - Fontana

May 1992
Ocean Colour Scene - album - Fontana

June 1992
Do Yourself a Favour - single - Fontana

February 1996
The Riverboat Song - single - MCA

March 1996
You've Got It Bad - single - MCA

April 1996 -
Moseley Shoals - album - MCA

June 1996
The Day We Caught the Train - MCA

May 1997
B-Sides, Seasides And Freerides - album - MCA

Sources

CHAPTER 1	**NME/Q Magazine/Record Collector/Time Out**
CHAPTER 2	**Arena Magazine/NME/ Q Magazine/Record Collector/ Vox Magazine/Time Out**
CHAPTER 3	**Q Magazine/NME/Record Collector/Select Magazine**
CHAPTER 4	**Mojo magazine, Jim irvin/NME/Q Magazine/Record Collector/ Sky Magazine/Time Out/Vox Magazine**
CHAPTER 5	**The Express/NME/Record Collector/Select Magazine/Sky Magazine**

Ocean Colour Scene

Ocean Colour Scene
Ocean Colour Scene
Ocean Colour Scene

Ocean
Colour
Scene

Ocean
Colour
Scene